Clinical
and
Investigative Features
of
Cardiac Pathology

Heart Failure

George C Sutton
Hillingdon Hospital, Middlesex, UK

Kim M Fox
National Heart Hospital, London, UK

John Bayliss
National Heart Hospital, London, UK

Current Medical Literature Ltd, London

Acknowledgments

The authors are grateful to John Swales, Professor of Medicine, University of Leicester, for the section on Hypertension and to John Davies, Royal Gwent Hospital, for his help on the section dealing with Restrictive Cardiomyopathy.

The authors also gratefully acknowledge the contributions of Michael Davies, Simon Rees, Robert Anderson, Stuart Hunter, Ian Kerr, Graham Leech, Fergus McCartney, Michael Rigby and the authors, editors and contributors to the following publications:

The Slide Atlas of Cardiology and Supplement (Sutton, Anderson and Fox. Medi-Cine Ltd, 1978 and 1986)

Physiological and Clinical Aspects of Cardiac Auscultation (Harris, Sutton, Towers. Medi-Cine Ltd. 1976)

An Introduction to Echocardiography (Leech, Kisslo. Medi-Cine Productions, 1981)

An Introduction to Nuclear Cardiology (Walton, Ell. Current Medical Literature, 1985)

An Introduction to Cardiovascular Digital Subtraction Angiography (Hunter, Walton, Hunter. Current Medical Literature, 1987)

An Introduction to Magnetic Resonance of the Cardiovascular System (Underwood, Firman. Current Medical Literature, 1987)

Published by Current Medical Literature Ltd,
40–42 Osnaburgh Street, London,
NW1 3ND, U.K.

ISBN 1850090858

Clinical
and
Investigative Features
of
Cardiac Pathology

Monograph Series

Note
The small images which accompany the text at the beginning of each chapter appear later in the chapter in a larger format.

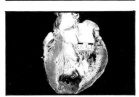

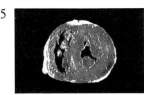

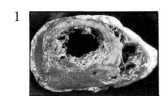

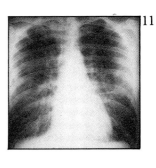

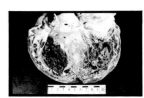

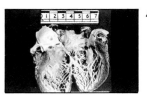

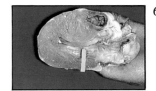

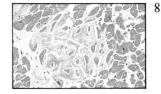

The clinical syndrome of heart failure consists of breathlessness, evidence of poor tissue perfusion (fatigue, oliguria, drowsiness) and the consequences of stimulation of the sympathetic and renin-angiotensin-aldosterone systems (tachycardia, peripheral vasoconstriction, salt and water retention). The clinical features of heart failure may be caused by impairment of myocardial function or a structural abnormality. Investigation of the patient is necessary in order to determine the cardiac abnormality which has given rise to the clinical syndrome of heart failure.

The commonest pathological abnormality of the heart which gives rise to the clinical syndrome of heart failure is disease of the myocardium. Other causes such as valvular heart disease, congenital heart disease and pericardial disease will not be discussed in this text. In ischaemic heart disease (acute myocardial infarction [1] and chronic ischaemic myocardial damage [2] including left ventricular aneurysm [3]) and dilated cardiomyopathy [4], left ventricular dysfunction may be both systolic and diastolic. Myocardial dysfunction is predominantly diastolic in hypertensive heart disease, hypertrophic cardiomyopathy [5,6] and restrictive cardiomyopathy (e.g. endomyocardial fibrosis [7]). Other causes include specific heart-muscle disease such as alcohol related cardiomyopathy, myocarditis and thyroid disease which cause clinical syndromes indistinguishable from dilated cardiomyopathy. Amyloidosis [8] causes a syndrome similar to restrictive cardiomyopathy. High output states such as Paget's disease, arterio-venous fistula, anaemia and Beri-Beri can result in heart failure. Right ventricular dysfunction may accompany left ventricular dysfunction. Any cause of pulmonary hypertension, either acute (massive pulmonary embolism [9]) or chronic (chronic obstructive airways disease, primary pulmonary hypertension, chronic thrombo-embolic disease) may result in right ventricular myocardial dysfunction and clinical heart failure.

Symptoms

Acute heart failure presents with acute breathlessness and lack of perfusion of vital organs. Breathlessness is mainly caused by pulmonary congestion due to increased left ventricular filling pressure. Lying flat increases pulmonary venous pressure further and causes orthopnoea; this may progress to the development of frank pulmonary oedema causing attacks of breathlessness at night which wake the patient (paroxysmal nocturnal dyspnoea). Unlike acute heart failure the cause of breathlessness in chronic heart failure is less well understood, but is probably more related to reduced perfusion of the tissues than to pulmonary congestion. Occasionally, a non-productive cough may be the only symptom in heart failure. Pulmonary oedema is often incorrectly diagnosed as bronchitis. Fatigue in chronic heart failure is mainly due to the reduced cardiac reserve on exercise and inadequate blood flow to exercising muscles.

Acute heart failure may be precipitated by an alteration of cardiac rhythm in patients with pre-existing myocardial dysfunction, fresh damage to the myocardium (e.g. myocardial infarction or myocarditis), inappropriate alterations of therapy and rarely, infection or pulmonary infarction. Occasionally, no precipitating cause can be found.

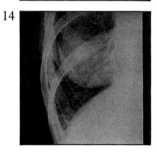

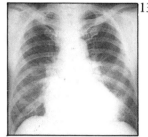

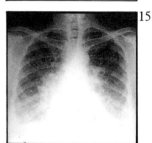

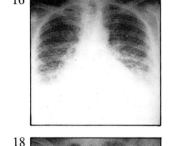

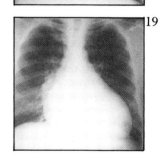

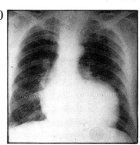

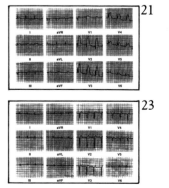

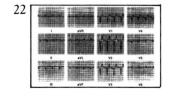

Patients with chronic heart failure may notice the development of fluid retention with swollen ankles and abdominal distention due to ascites or hepatic congestion. The patient with chronic heart failure may complain of nausea, vomiting and loss of weight due to gastrointestinal and hepatic congestion; such patients are frequently thought to have other abdominal pathology.

Acute right ventricular failure due to massive pulmonary embolism presents with circulatory collapse or acute breathlessness.

Signs

The physical signs may indicate whether heart failure is due to myocardial dysfunction or some other abnormality. Myocardial dysfunction renders the ventricles stiff and gives rise to a double apical impulse, a gallop rhythm (fourth and/or third heart sound) and secondary mitral or tricuspid regurgitation (pansystolic murmur); primary valvular abnormalities, congenital cardiac abnormalities or pericardial disease have distinctive clinical features.

Low cardiac output with stimulation of the sympathetic and renin-angiotensin-aldosterone systems will be associated with sinus tachycardia, peripheral vasoconstriction and fluid retention, causing a raised jugular venous pressure, pulmonary oedema, hepatic congestion, ascites and peripheral oedema. Renal, hepatic and cerebral impairment may also occur.

Investigations

Investigation of patients with clinical heart failure is essential in order to diagnose the cause. Valvular, congenital and pericardial disease may be detected but will not be discussed further in this section.

Radiology

In patients presenting with 'acute' heart failure and breathlessness, the heart size may be normal [10,11] or enlarged. An enlarged heart implies pre-existing heart disease. The chest X-ray will show evidence of raised pulmonary venous pressure, such as dilatation of the upper zone pulmonary vessels, left atrial enlargement [12], Kerley B-lines (short horizontal lines in the peripheral lung fields [13,14]) and occasionally, unilateral or bilateral pleural effusions [15]; these findings correlate well with the elevation of left ventricular filling pressure and left atrial pressure and the consequent high pulmonary capillary wedge pressure. Pulmonary oedema is usually bilateral [16] but, occasionally, may be unilateral [17]. In 'chronic' heart failure the heart is usually enlarged and there may [18] or may not [19] be radiological features associated with raised pulmonary venous pressure. Characteristic radiological abnormalities are seen in acute pulmonary embolism, cor pulmonale, primary pulmonary hypertension and chronic thromboembolic disease. Features suggestive of a left ventricular aneurysm may also be seen [20].

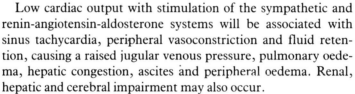

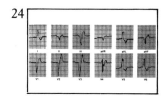

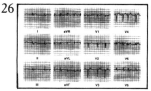

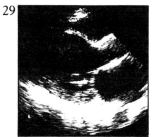

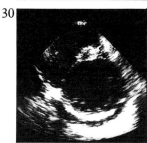

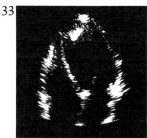

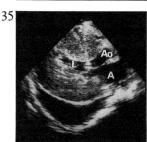

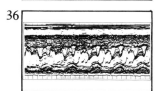

Electrocardiography

A normal ECG should alert the clinician to the possibility that the diagnosis of myocardial failure is incorrect. The ECG may show acute [21] or old [22] myocardial infarction, or evidence of left ventricular aneurysm [23]. Common abnormalities associated with chronic left ventricular dysfunction include left atrial configuration of the 'P' waves, left bundle branch block [24] or only ST/T abnormalities [25]. Patients with heart failure due to myocardial disease often have rhythm abnormalities which may be seen on the routine ECG [26,27] or may be detected only during 24 hour ambulatory monitoring [28]. Right ventricular dysfunction may be associated with right axis deviation and right bundle branch block or evidence of right ventricular hypertrophy.

Echocardiography

The echocardiographic features will reflect the underlying cardiac abnormality. In patients with ischaemic heart disease, 2-dimensional echocardiography will show an increase in left ventricular dimensions and reduction in wall motion which may be either regional [29,30] or generalized [31]. Systolic wall thinning and/or dyskinesia are readily apparent from inspection of the systolic and diastolic images. A localized left ventricular aneurysm may be detected by 2-dimensional echocardiography [32] and thrombus within an abnormal ventricle may sometimes be seen [33]. In patients with dilated cardiomyopathy not due to ischaemic heart disease, the left ventricular dimensions are again increased and amplitude of wall motion is reduced globally [34]. Slight enlargement of the left atrium, due to chronic elevation of the left ventricular filling pressure, is common.

In hypertrophic cardiomyopathy there is marked left ventricular hypertrophy which may be concentric [35] or predominantly affecting the septum [36] or only the apex. The left ventricular cavity is small and may become obliterated in systole. Systolic anterior motion (SAM) of the anterior mitral valve leaflet may be seen [36] and there may be left atrial enlargement.

In restrictive cardiomyopathy, 2-dimensional echocardiography is helpful in the early diagnosis. Specific cavity changes such as apical and endocardial thickening can be demonstrated. Myocardial infiltration (e.g. endomyocardial fibrosis) gives a particular diagnostic reflection pattern on the grey scale and this can be further enhanced by amplitude process, colour-encoded tissue characterization techniques [37].

In patients with right heart failure due to pulmonary hypertension there may be evidence of paradoxical septal motion on M-mode echocardiography, and right ventricular hypertrophy and dilatation will be seen by 2-dimensional echocardiography.

In patients with hypertensive heart disease, 2-dimensional echocardiography may show a hypertrophied but normally contracting left ventricle with diastolic dysfunction, but in more advanced disease, hypertrophy with a dilated and poorly contracting ventricle is seen.

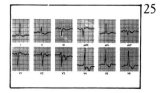

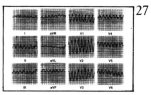

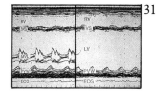

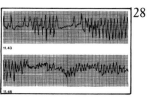

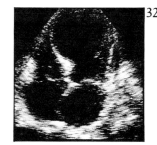

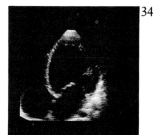

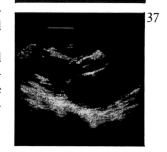

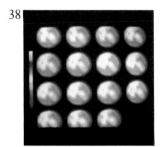

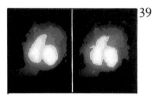

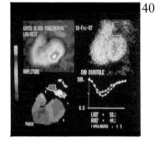

Nuclear Techniques

Ventricular function may be assessed using first pass angiocardiography or, more commonly, by equilibrium-gated blood pool scintigraphy. Imaging of the technetium-99m labelled blood pool within the cardiac chambers is performed dynamically by 'gating' data into 16, 32 or 64 frames per cardiac cycle [38]; computer analysis of these raw data permits assessment of ventricular chamber volumes [39]. More sophisticated analysis can generate volume curves and ejection fraction [40]. The changes in spatial information during the cardiac cycle can be used to generate colour-encoded images representing the amplitude and phase of regional wall motion (parametric imaging). This can demonstrate clearly any discoordinate and dyskinetic zones [41–43].

Regional myocardial perfusion abnormalities causing heart failure may be assessed by thallium-201 scintigraphy. A defect in thallium uptake on exercise which normalizes on reperfusion during recovery is indicative of exercise-induced ischaemia [44–46]. Thallium defects which persist at rest indicate an area of myocardial infarction [47].

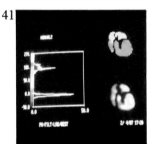

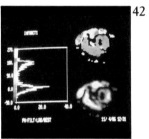

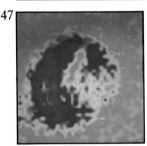

Cardiac Catheterization and Angiography

Bedside monitoring of right heart, haemodynamic variables can be useful in the management of patients with acute heart failure. A ballon-tipped thermodilution catheter [48] positioned with its tip in the pulmonary artery [49] allows accurate measurement of pulmonary artery and wedge pressure and cardiac output, facilitating accurate diagnosis.

In heart failure due to left ventricular disease, the left ventricular end-diastolic pressure is usually elevated, often with a prominent 'a' wave [50]. In hypertrophic cardiomyopathy, intracavity recordings may reveal left ventricular mid-cavity obstruction; restrictive cardiomyopathy causes characteristic haemodynamic abnormalities [51].

Left ventricular angiography is often unnecessary in patients with heart failure as non-invasive techniques will have defined the nature and degree of dysfunction. Localized hypokinesis [52] or left ventricular aneurysm may be seen following myocardial infarction. Alternatively, the left ventricle may be globally hypokinetic in generalized ischaemic heart disease or dilated cardiomyopathy [53]. Gross hypertrophy and systolic cavity obliteration is seen in hypertrophic cardiomyopathy [54]. Cavity obliteration and atrioventricular valvar regurgitation is also seen in restrictive cardiomyopathy [55].

Coronary arteriography is performed to demonstrate whether heart failure is due to coronary artery disease and, if so, to assess the possibilities of treatment. Localized stenoses [56] or, more often, widespread coronary disease may be found [57] even in the absence of a history of myocardial infarction or angina.

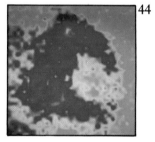

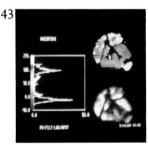

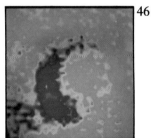

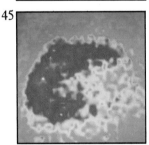

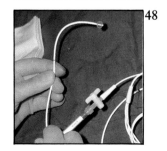

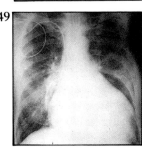

Exercise Testing

All the investigations referred to above assess the type and degree of left ventricular dysfunction rather than the clinical state of the patient. Exercise testing proves an objective measure of function-

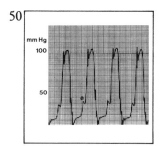

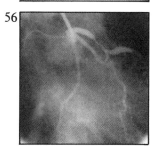

al impairment in heart failure. Maximal or submaximal tests on a treadmill or bicycle ergometer, with measurement of exercise time or oxygen consumption [58] can be useful in the diagnosis and follow up of symptomatic patients.

Magnetic Resonance Imaging

Magnetic resonance images are maps of the radio signals emitted by the photons within the body (mainly those in water and fat) under the influence of a powerful magnetic field. They reveal cardiac anatomy noninvasively and without the injection of contrast media. Accurate measurements of ventricular volumes [59], wall thickness [60a & 60b] and wall motion [61] can be made, and filling defects such as thrombus are readily detected. The images can be acquired as cine loops to demonstrate moving anatomy, and the turbulence of valvular disease and intracardiac shunting can be encoded in the phase of the magnetic resonance signal. Cine velocity mapping holds great potential for the assessment of vascular disease.

In patients with heart failure, the main application of magnetic resonance imaging is in the accurate measurement and follow up of ventricular function, the detection of thrombus, and the assessment of associated lesions such as mitral regurgitation.

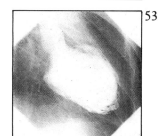

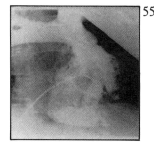

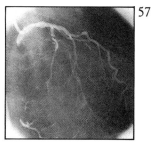

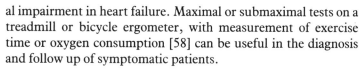

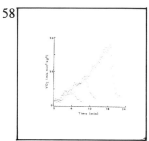

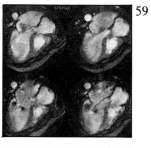

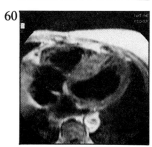

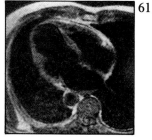

1 Transverse slice (fresh) of the ventricles. A recent (four-day-old) full-thickness myocardial infarction is present in the anterior wall of the left ventricle which extends into the interventricular septum.

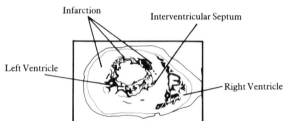

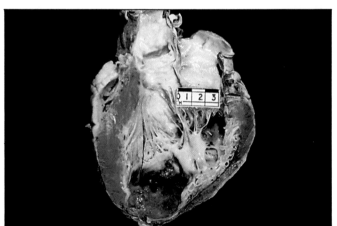

2 Widespread ischaemic scarring of the myocardium producing a dilated thin-walled ventricle. A thrombus has formed in one area in relation to the aneurysmal bulge of the ventricular wall.

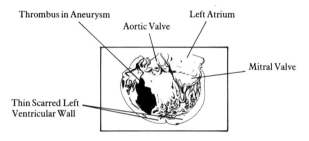

3 Localized left ventricular aneurysm due to previous myocardial infarction. The aneurysm does not contain more than a fine deposit of thrombus and has a larger central cavity opening into the ventricle.

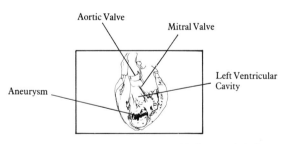

4 Dilated cardiomyopathy: the opened left ventricle has a large cavity and thin wall.

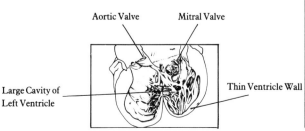

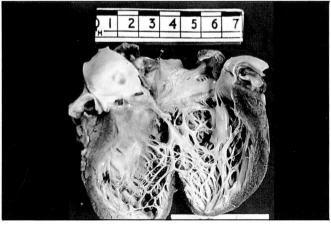

5 Transverse section through heart in hypertrophic cardiomyopathy showing concentric left ventricular hypertrophy.

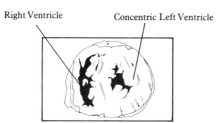

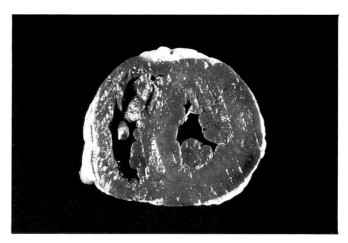

6 The left ventricle from a patient with hypertrophic cardiomyopathy showing a small cavity with very thick wall. The septal region is asymmetrically thickened being at least twice as thick as the parietal wall. The septum bulges into the outflow tract of the left ventricle and impinges onto the anterior cusp of the mitral valve (arrow).

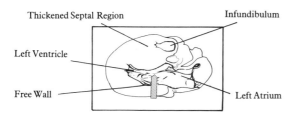

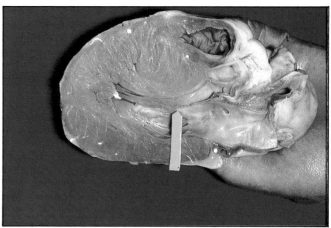

7 Section through the left ventricle in endomyocardial fibrosis. There is marked left ventricular apical obliteration with endocardial thickening and super-added thrombus.

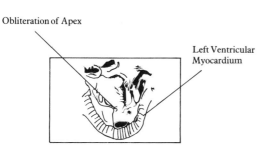

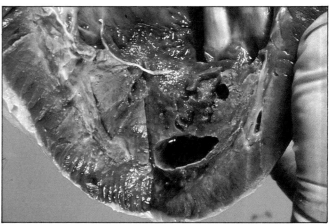

8 Amyloid deposition in the myocardium. In haematoxylin and eosin stained histological sections amyloid is a pale pink homogeneous material. Amyloid (arrows) is laid down between myocardial cells and ultimately completely surrounds them leaving a lattice of amyloid within which a few residual muscle cells are embedded, staining a deeper pink colour.

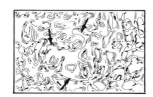

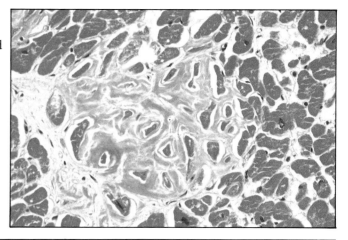

9 Large saddle embolus is seen astride both right and left pulmonary arteries.

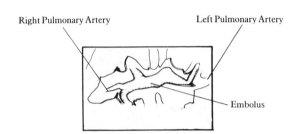

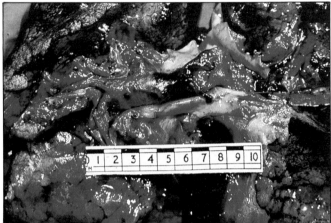

10 Chest radiograph showing a normal sized heart with upper lobe venous distention and a small right pleural effusion, due to recent myocardial infarction.

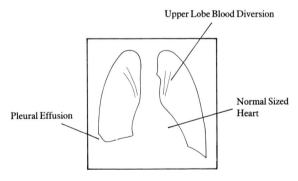

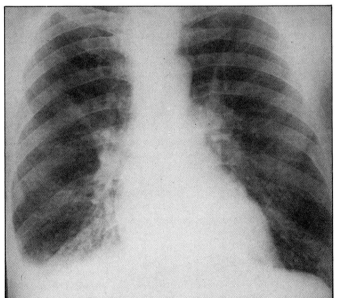

11 Chest radiograph showing a normal sized heart with pulmonary oedema.

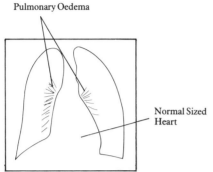

Pulmonary Oedema

Normal Sized Heart

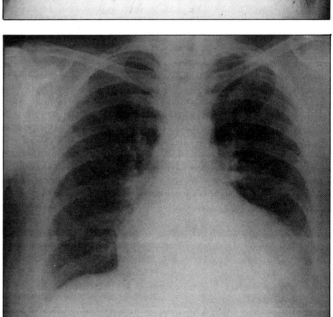

12 Chest radiograph showing large heart and left atrium with pulmonary venous hypertension.

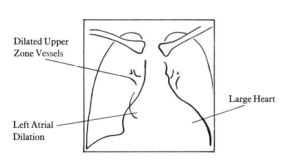

Dilated Upper Zone Vessels

Large Heart

Left Atrial Dilation

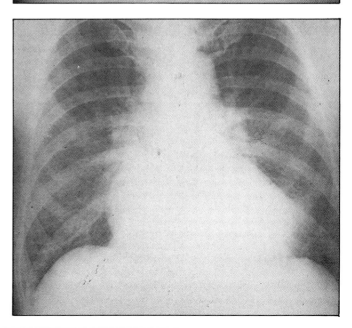

13 Chest radiograph showing cardiomegaly, upper lobe pulmonary venous distention and Kerley B-lines.

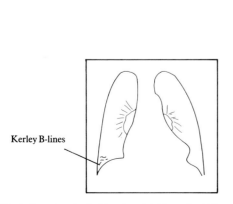

Kerley B-lines

14 Detail from chest radiograph showing septal lines and pleural effusion.

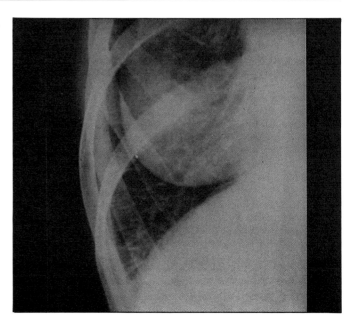

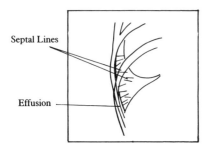

15 Chest radiograph showing pulmonary oedema and bilateral pleural effusions following acute myocardial infarction.

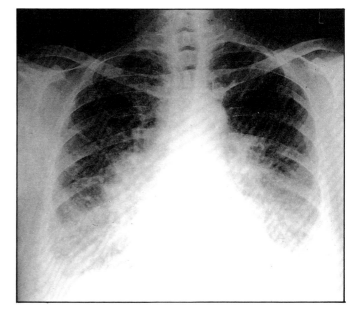

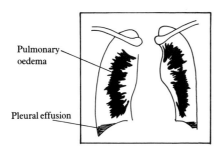

16 Chest radiograph in acute heart failure due to acute myocardial infarction. There is gross pulmonary oedema.

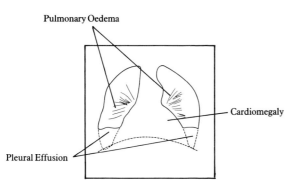

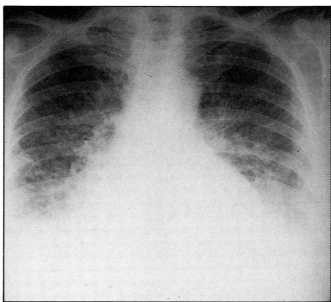

17 Chest radiograph showing cardiomegaly and pulmonary oedema of the right lung only.

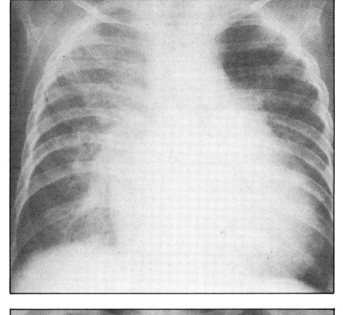

Unilateral Pulmonary Oedema

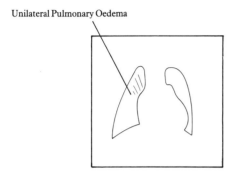

18 Chest radiograph showing cardiomegaly with features of raised pulmonary venous pressure (enlarged veins and upper zone blood diversion).

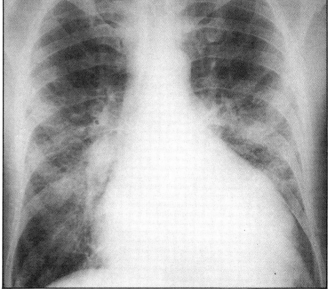

Enlarged Pulmonary Veins

Cardiomegaly

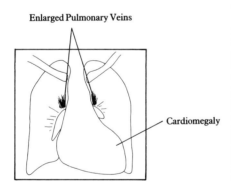

19 Chest radiograph showing an enlarged heart without upper zone blood diversion.

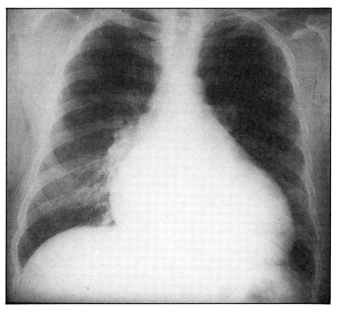

Enlarged Heart

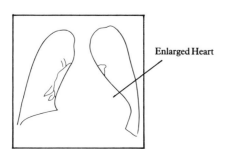

20 Chest radiograph showing a bulge on the left heart
border suggestive of a left ventricular aneurysm.

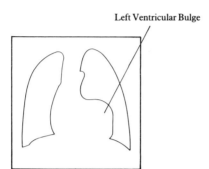

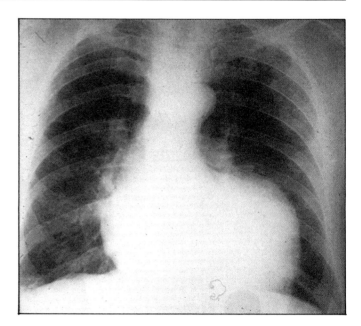

21

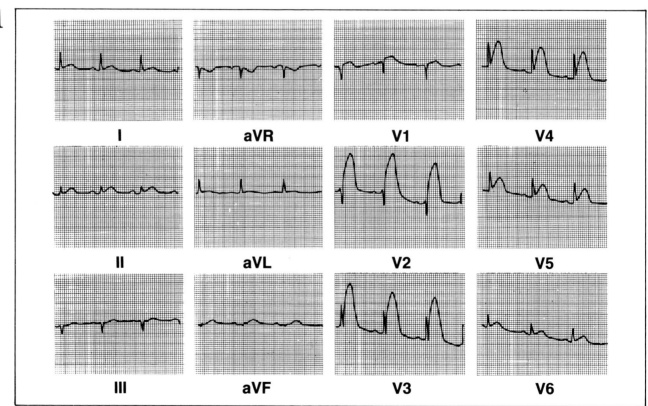

I	aVR	V1	V4
II	aVL	V2	V5
III	aVF	V3	V6

Electrocardiogram showing the very early changes of anterior myocardial infarction (30 min after onset of pain).
There is ST elevation in leads I, II, and across all the V leads, but no Q wave development yet.

22

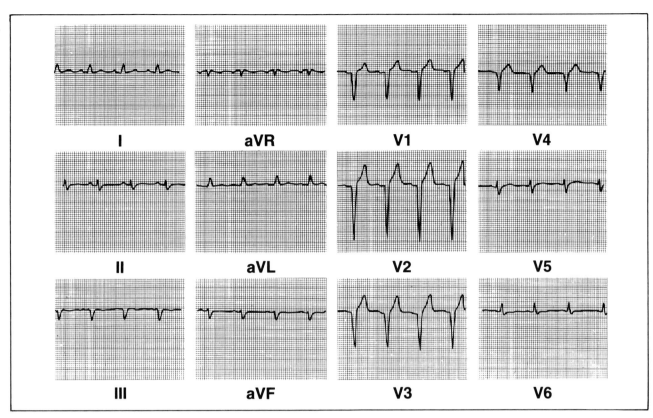

Electrocardiogram of a patient with chronic ischaemic heart disease, showing old anterior infarction, with Q waves in V_{1-4} and poor R wave progression in V_{5-6}.

23

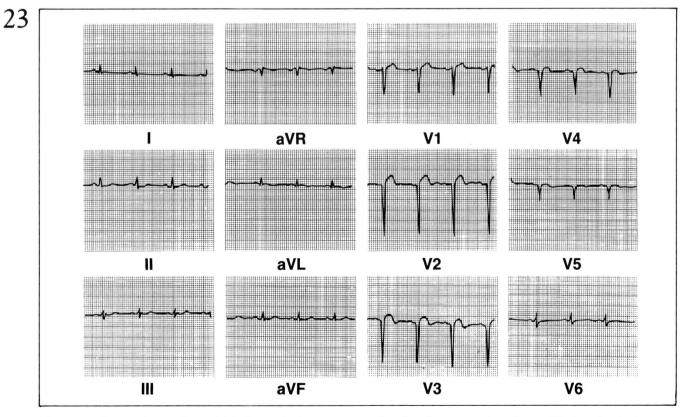

Electrocardiogram in a patient with left ventricular aneurysm, showing Q waves and persistent ST elevation in the anterior chest leads, six months after myocardial infarction.

24

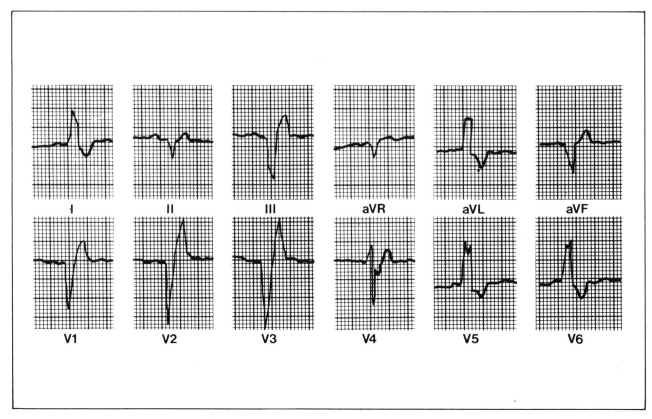

Electrocardiogram in a patient with dilated cardiomyopathy showing left bundle branch block.

25

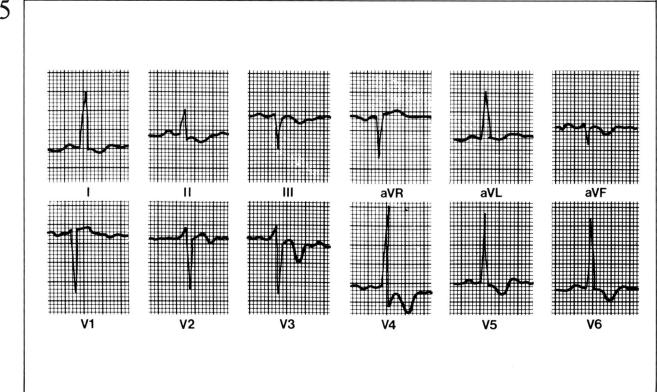

Electrocardiogram in a patient with dilated cardiomyopathy showing non-specific ST/T abnormalities.

26

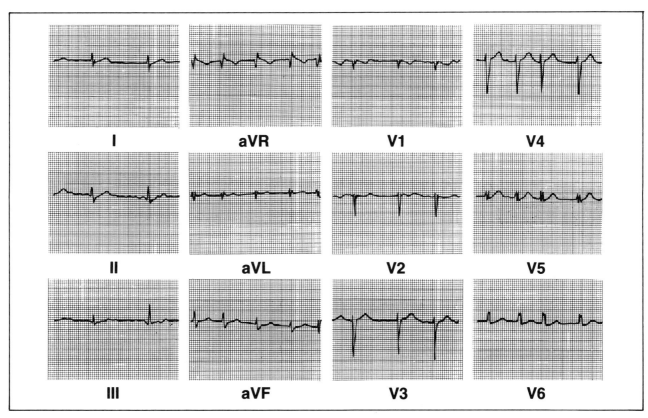

Electrocardiogram of a patient with dilated cardiomyopathy, showing atrial fibrillation, poor R wave progression in the chest leads, and partial left bundle branch block, but no Q waves.

27

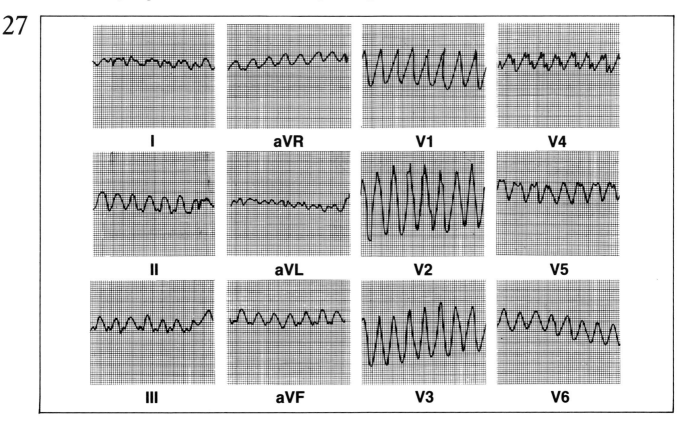

Electrocardiogram recorded from a patient with dilated cardiomyopathy, taken when he complained of dizziness. The 12 lead ECG shows ventricular tachycardia.

28

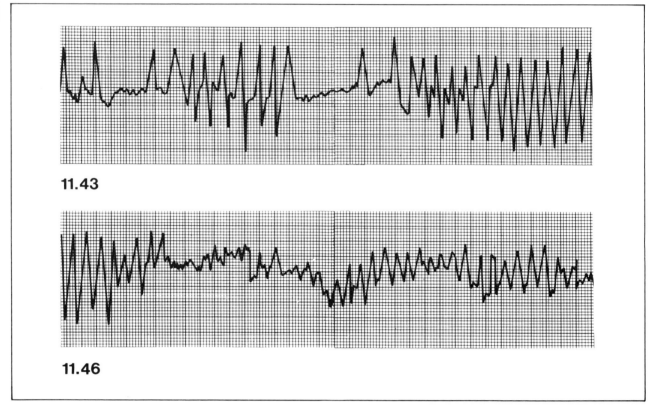

11.43

11.46

Ambulatory ECG recording from a patient with heart failure. On returning home with the recorder at 11.35, the patient sat down to drink a cup of coffee. At 11.43 he developed ventricular tachycardia and collapsed. At 11.46 ventricular fibrillation developed and the patient died.

29

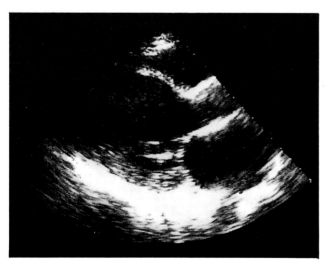
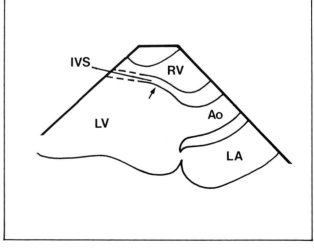

2-D echocardiographic systolic long axis view in a patient with septal infarction showing thinning of the septum (arrow) bulging into the right ventricle.

30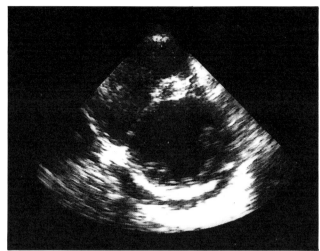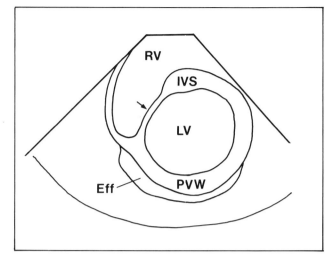

2-D echocardiographic systolic short axis view at level of papillary muscles in a patient with septal infarction. There is thinning of the septum (arrow) in relation to the anterior wall, and there is a pericardial effusion.

31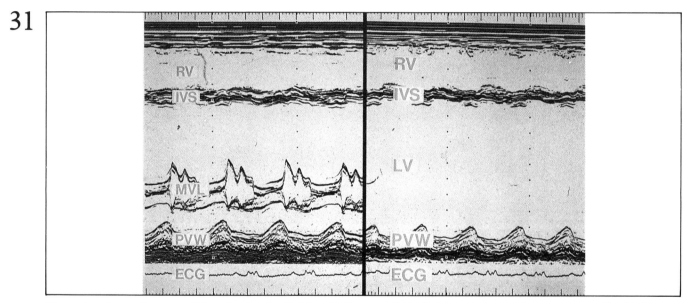

M-mode echocardiogram of the mitral valve (left) and left ventricle (right) in a patient with severe generalized left ventricular dysfunction due to coronary artery disease.

32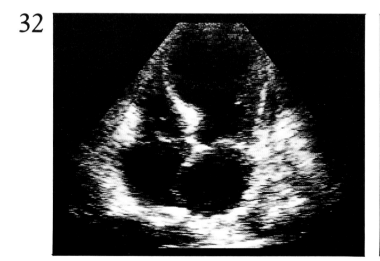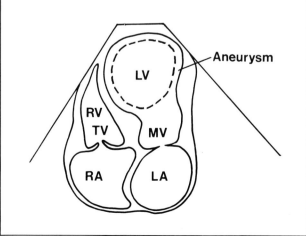

2-D echocardiographic apical four-chamber view showing a large left ventricular aneurysm.

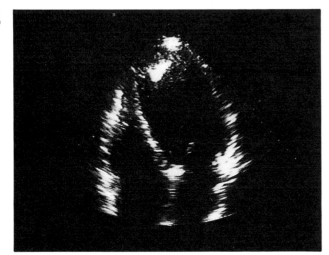 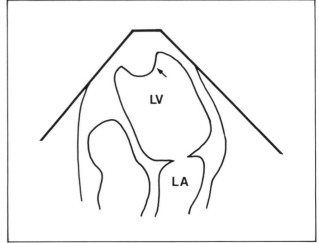

2-D echocardiographic apical four-chamber view showing apical thrombus (arrow) in a patient with an old apical myocardial infarction.

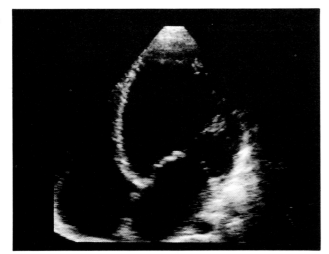 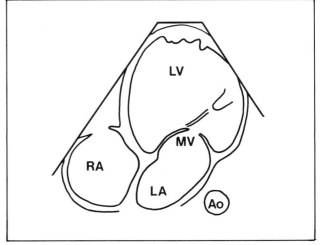

2-D echocardiographic apical four-chamber view showing left ventricular dilatation in dilated cardiomyopathy. Note the thin-walled globular left ventricle. The irregularities in the apex may be due to mural thrombus.

 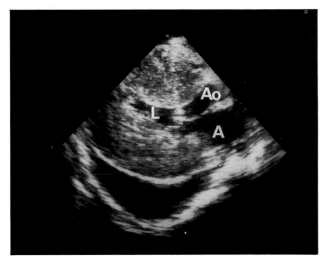 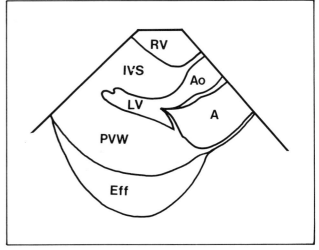

2-D echocardiographic parasternal long axis systolic view in hypertrophic cardiomyopathy with gross symmetrical hypertrophy of the left ventricle and slit-like cavity. Note additional pericardial effusion.

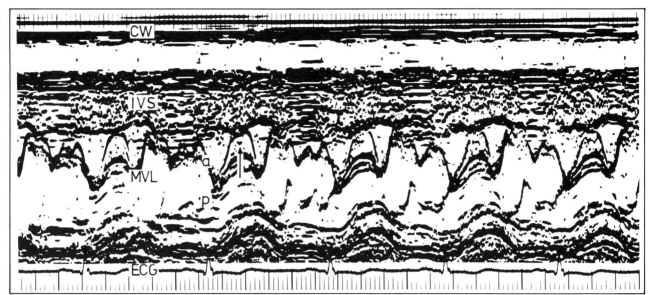

M-mode echocardiogram of hypertrophic cardiomyopathy with left ventricular outflow obstruction. The echocardiogram shows systolic anterior movement of the anterior leaflet (arrowed) which also strikes the septum at the onset of diastole.

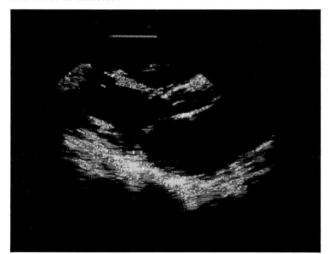
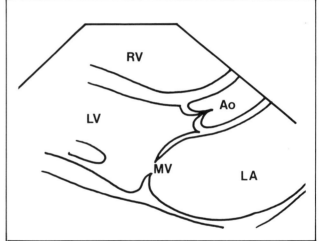

2-D echocardiographic amplitude processed colour-encoded long axis parasternal view in endomyocardial fibrosis showing increased echo density and endocardial thickening on the posterior left ventricular wall, thickening and tethering of the posterior mitral valve leaflet and left atrial dilatation.

38 Gated blood pool scan in a normal subject : 16 frames have been acquired (end systole at frame 4, end diastole at frame 1).

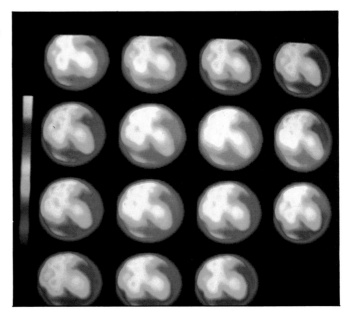

39 Gated blood pool scan in dilated cardiomyopathy showing little difference in the size of the ventricular cavities between end-diastole (left) and end-systole (right).

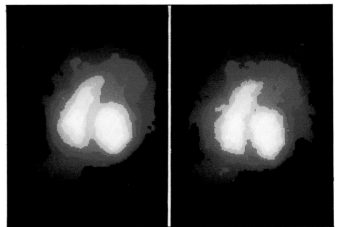

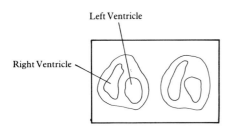

40 End-diastolic frames of equilibrium gated blood pool scans (top right) with regions of interest outlining the right and left ventricular cavities. By measuring the counts in these regions throughout the cardiac cycle, an accurate measure of the change in cavity volume can be made, to yield volume curves and calculated ejection fractions (EF) (bottom right);
a) Normal (LVEF 58%, RVEF 44%),
b) LV aneurysm (LVEF 23%, RVEF 24%),
c) Dilated cardiomyopathy (LVEF 10%, RVEF 11%).

(a)

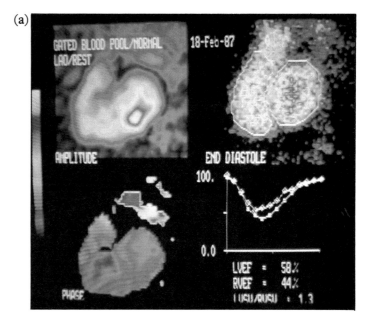

(b)

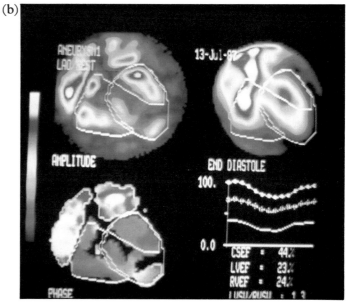

(c)

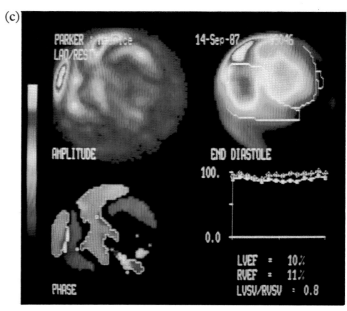

41 Parametric imaging. By constructing volume curves throughout the cardiac cycle from each pixel of a gated blood pool scan, the computer can generate colour-encoded images of amplitude of regional wall motion, and phase of wall motion. In this normal heart the amplitude image (bottom right) shows vigorous left ventricular contraction. The phase image (top right) shows both ventricles contract uniformly and in synchrony (coded blue), with the atria 180° out of phase (i.e. contract in diastole) (coded red), giving two sharp peaks at 0° and 180° on the phase histogram.

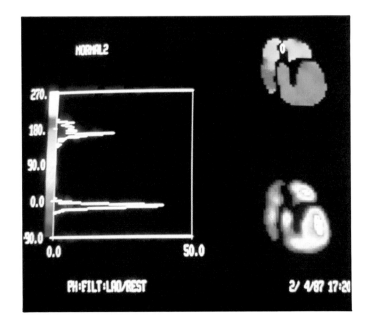

42 Parametric images following myocardial infarction. The amplitude image reveals poor amplitude of left ventricular wall motion. The phase image is fragmented, showing discoordinate ventricular contraction, giving poorly defined peaks on the phase histogram.

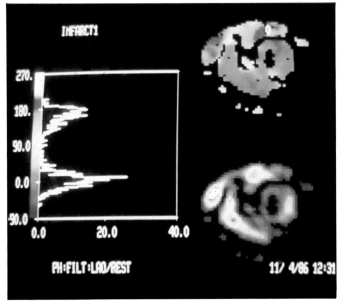

43 Parametric images from a patient with left ventricular aneurysm. The amplitude image shows reduced apical movement and the phase image shows clearly that motion of the apex is out of phase compared to the rest of the ventricle.

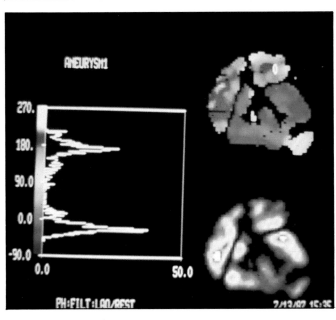

44

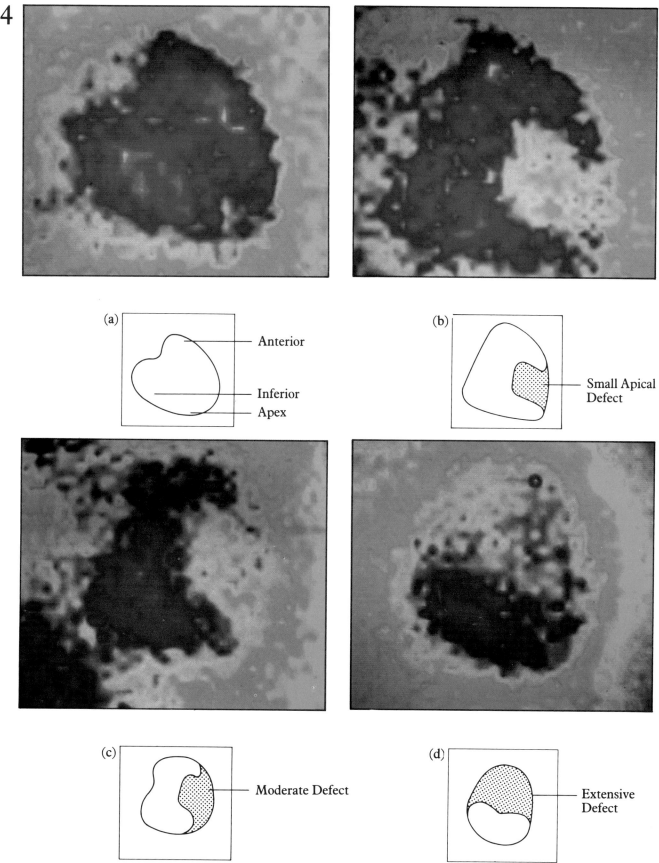

(a) Anterior — Inferior — Apex

(b) Small Apical Defect

(c) Moderate Defect

(d) Extensive Defect

Thallium-201 scintigraphy, antero-posterior projection, recorded immediately after exercise; a) normal appearance, b) small apical defect, c) moderate anterior and apical defects, d) extensive defect affecting the whole of the anterior wall and apex.

45

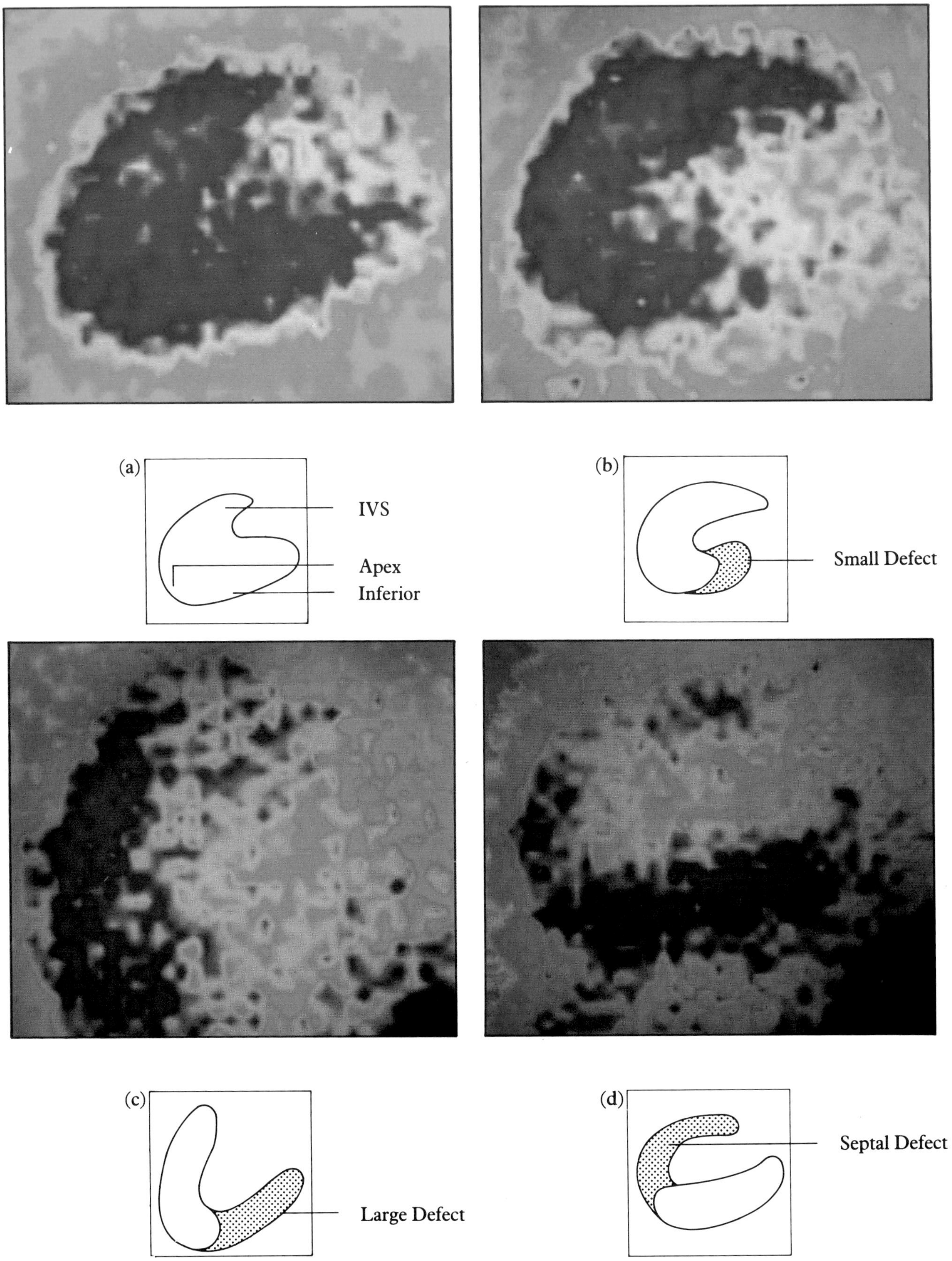

(a)

IVS

Apex

Inferior

(b)

Small Defect

(c)

Large Defect

(d)

Septal Defect

Thallium-201 scintigraphy, lateral projection, recorded immediately after exercise; a) normal appearance, b) small infero-posterior defect, c) large inferior defect, d) septal defect.

46

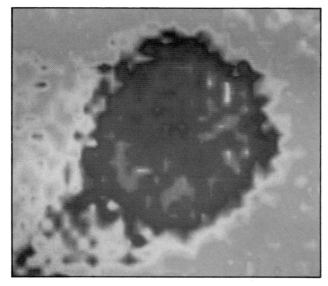
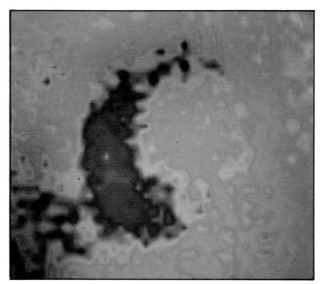

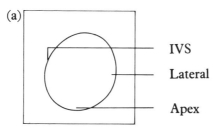
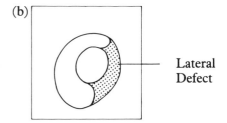

(a)

IVS

Lateral

Apex

(b)

Lateral
Defect

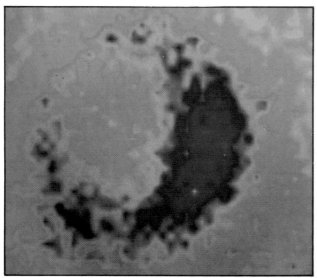

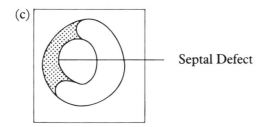

(c)

Septal Defect

Thallium-201 scintigraphy, left anterior oblique projection, recorded immediately after exercise; a) normal appearance, b) lateral defect. The left ventricular cavity is dilated, c) and there is a septal defect.

47 Thallium-201 scintigraphy, left anterior oblique projection. Upper panel shows resting scintigram which is essentially normal apart from a small lateral defect. Lower panel shows scintigram recorded immediately after exercise in the same patient with a large lateral defect.

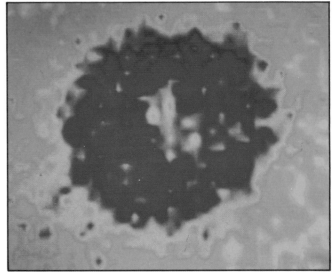

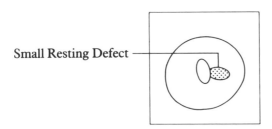

Small Resting Defect

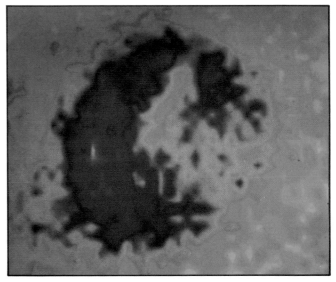

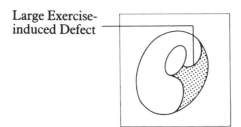

Large Exercise-induced Defect

48 A balloon-tipped thermodilution catheter for right heart haemodynamic monitoring.

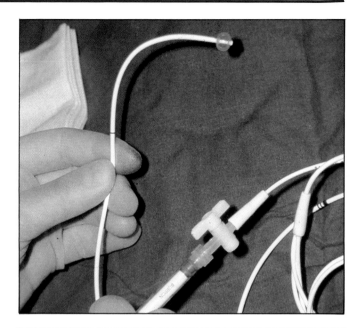

49 Chest radiograph showing a catheter inserted via the right subclavian vein, positioned with its tip in the right pulmonary artery for measurement of wedge pressure.

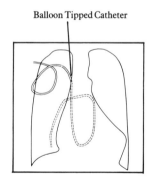

Balloon Tipped Catheter

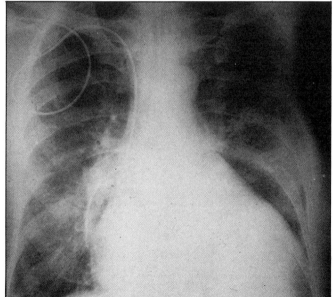

50 Pressure recording from the left ventricle in a patient with heart failure. The end-diastolic pressure is raised and there is a prominent 'a' wave.

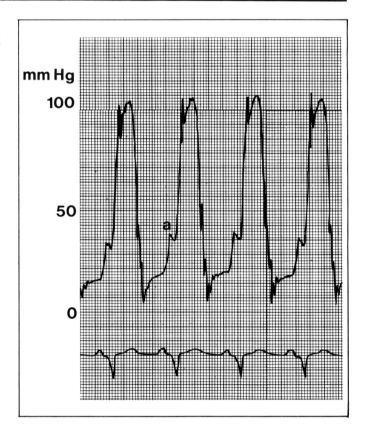

51 Pressure recordings taken from the right and left ventricles simultaneously in endomyocardial fibrosis showing the typical 'dip and plateau' and the elevated and different end diastolic pressure measurements.

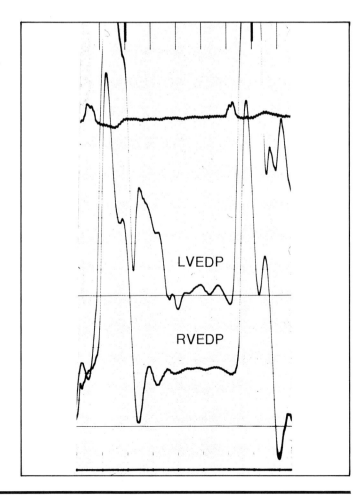

52

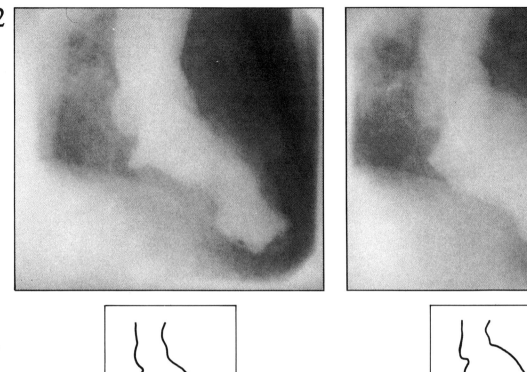

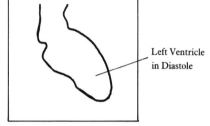

Left Ventricle
in Systole   Dyskinetic Area

Left Ventricle
in Diastole

Left ventricular angiogram in the right anterior oblique projection. Systolic (left) and diastolic (right) frames reveal presence of apical dyskinesis and thrombus.

53

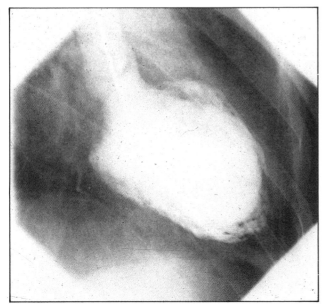 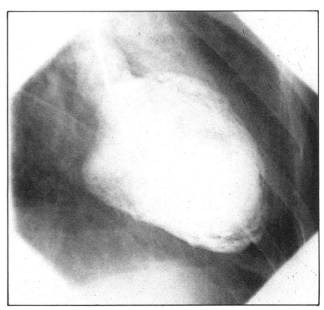

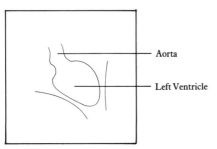

Aorta

Left Ventricle

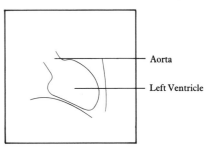

Aorta

Left Ventricle

Left ventricular angiogram in the right anterior oblique projection with systolic (left) and diastolic (right) frames showing global hypokinesis and ventricular dilatation.

54 Left ventricular angiogram in hypertrophic cardiomyopathy showing in systole (antero-posterior projection) a small irregular cavity.

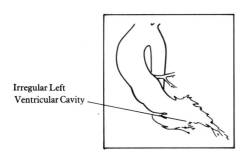

Irregular Left
 Ventricular Cavity

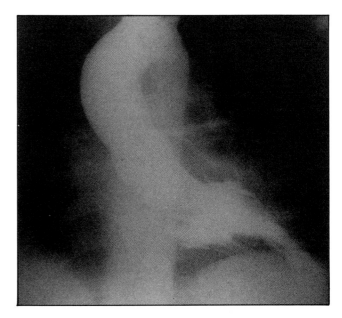

55 Right ventricular angiogram showing apical cavity obliteration and tricuspid regurgitation due to endomyocardial fibrosis.

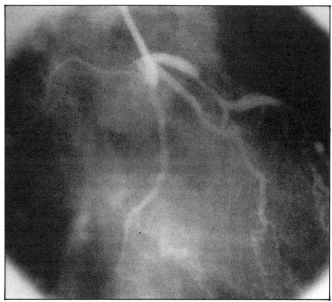

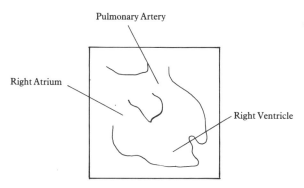

56 Coronary arteriogram (right anterior oblique projection) showing a long severe narrowing of the left anterior descending coronary artery.

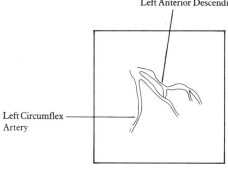

57 Coronary arteriogram (right anterior oblique projection) in three vessel coronary disease. The left coronary has been injected showing extensive disease, with retrograde filling of the right coronary artery.

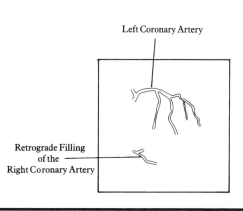

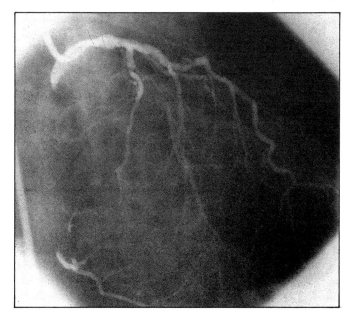

58 Oxygen consumption (VO_2) during symptom limited treadmill exercise and on recovery, in a normal subject (right), a patient with moderate heart failure (middle) and a patient with severe heart failure (left). At rest and during the first 5 minutes of exercise all three subjects have similar oxygen consumption, but peak VO_2 is progressively reduced with increasing heart failure.

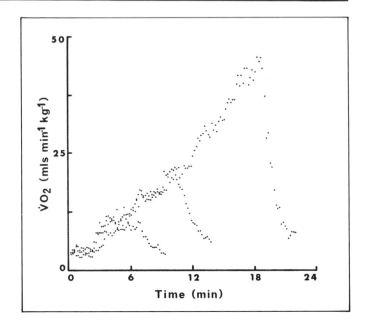

59 Magnetic resonance imaging in dilated cardiomyopathy. Four frames from a cine acquisition in the horizontal long axis plane using a field echo sequence where blood appears with high signal (white) except where there is turbulence. There is global left ventricular hypokinesia.

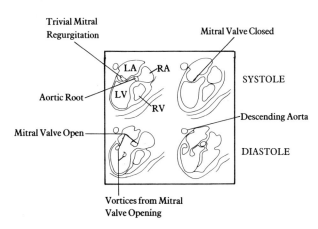

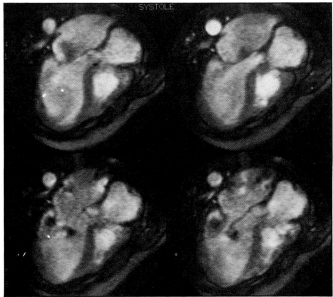

60 Magnetic resonance imaging in hypertrophic cardiomyopathy (HCM). Diastolic (a) and systolic (b) transverse sections showing asymmetric septal hypertrophy. The high signal from the septal myocardium is a consequence of altered relaxation times in the abnormal muscle.

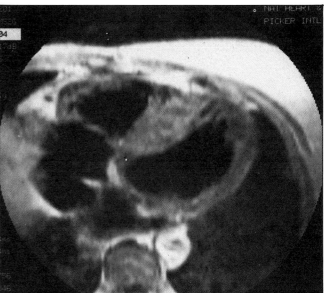

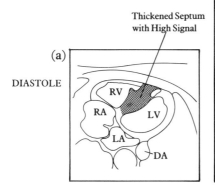

(a) DIASTOLE

Thickened Septum with High Signal

RV
RA
LV
LA
DA

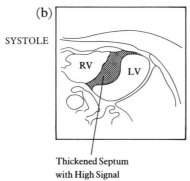

(b) SYSTOLE

RV
LV

Thickened Septum with High Signal

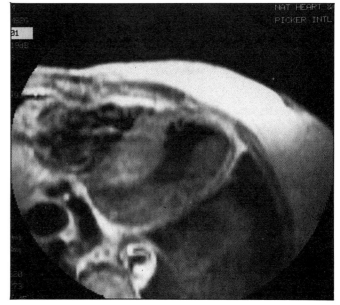

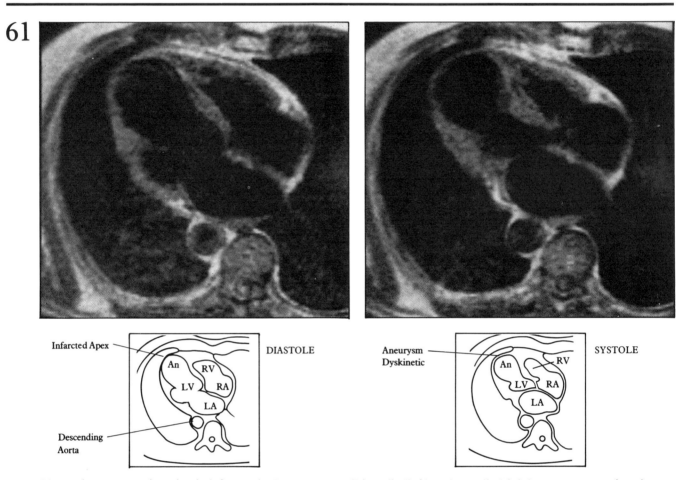

Magnetic resonance imaging in left ventricular aneurysm. Diastolic (left) and systolic (right) transverse sections in a patient with previous infarction and an apical left ventricular aneurysm. The basal myocardium contracts well whilst the apical myocardium is thin and dyskinetic.